TAKE CHARGE OF YOUR EMOTIONS:

Understanding the emotions of your teenagers

Kathleen G. Eucharia

Table of contents

Chapter 1

What are Emotions

Humans' reactions to events or circumstances, or their emotions, are known as emotions. The situation that causes an emotion determines the kind of feeling that an individual will feel. For instance, when someone hears excellent news, they are happy. When one feels threatened, one gets afraid. Emotions are produced subconsciously and characterize physiological conditions. They frequently include autonomous bodily responses to certain internal or external situations. Contrarily, feelings are conscious reflections and ideas that are inspired by individual emotional experiences.This indicates that while we may experience emotions without experiencing feelings, we simply cannot experience feelings without experiencing sensations.

There are as many purported emotions as there are divergent viewpoints among researchers. There are, roughly speaking, seven fundamental emotions: happiness, surprise, fear, disgust, anger, contempt, and sorrow.

We construct secondary emotions, which can total over 25, based on them. However, according to a new study from the University of Glasgow, there are just four fundamental facial expressions in humans as opposed to seven. However, this is just one debate thread that divides feelings into categories

Other researchers analyze emotional reactions using the two well-established orthogonal dimensions of arousal (excitement vs. tranquility) and valence (positivity vs. negativity). Any type of control of awareness, attention, and information processing involves arousal, which is the psycho-physiological condition of being awake and responsive to stimuli. However, one cannot assess the quality of emotion just based on the arousal component. The valence dimension addresses emotions of all types, whether they are positive (joy) or negative (fear).

Do feelings truly go unnoticed?
They are, indeed.

Consider the scenario of viewing a horror movie at home. Despite the fact that you are in a perfectly safe setting and there is nothing to be alarmed about, you could feel uneasy and worried. There's a chance you'll even make an effort to conceal yourself. Your body reacts by breathing more forcefully, beating your heart more quickly, and dilating your pupils more.

Your autonomous nervous system has already pulled the triggers and caused all bodily alterations before you can begin to become conscious of terror or even react with a scream. This demonstrates once more that sentiments do not always follow emotions, but that our actions are undoubtedly influenced by them.
Do emotions influence our thinking?

Our thinking can be somewhat influenced by our emotions. In short, our initial assessment of a novel scenario is constantly influenced by our sentiments, attitudes, and emotions. Therefore, Ron Richard writes in his essay about dispositions, attitudes, and habits, "our emotions are establishing the foundation for the thinking that is to come.

It's quite beneficial that emotions manifest "pre-cognitively," or before thinking. There is just no time to contemplate when threats are imminent. Instead, emotions "take over" and in a matter of seconds, prompt quick behavioral reactions, averting undesirable results. Emotions aid in decision-making and provide inspiration for choosing and carrying out the right course of action.

Our daily lives are significantly impacted by our emotions. Depending on our emotions—happiness, rage, sadness, boredom, or frustration—we make choices. We pick interests and pastimes depending on the feelings they arouse. Knowing our emotions may make life easier and more stable for us to manage.

Feelings, emotions, and moods

The words emotions, feelings, and moods are frequently used interchangeably in ordinary speech, although they have diverse meanings. An emotion often lasts for a brief time yet is quite powerful. Additionally, emotions likely have a clear origin. For instance, you can feel angry after fighting with a buddy about football.

Feelings are what we experience as a result of emotions, which are responses to stimuli. The way we perceive a situation affects how we feel, which is why different people who are experiencing the same emotion may feel completely different things.

Consider the scenario of arguing with a buddy. Both of you could leave the conversation having felt the feeling of fury.

Because you believe your buddy never pays attention to you when you talk, your dissatisfaction may come out as hostility. On the other side, your friend's rage can come out as envy since they think you know a lot more than they do about the subject. Although you are both experiencing the same experience, due to your differing perceptions, your feelings are different.

Temporary emotional states are referred to as moods. Sometimes, emotions are brought on by blatant factors. For example, you could be in a good mood this week because you feel like everything is going your way.

However, it can sometimes be challenging to pinpoint the precise reason for a mood. For instance, you could discover that you've been depressed for a few days without knowing why. Speak with a doctor or a mental health expert about your worries if you've been experiencing a low mood or challenging emotions. They can help you get back to feeling your best by providing you with support, direction, and answers.

Just as for adults, emotional ups and downs are a typical part of growing up.

Teenagers frequently experience mixed emotions, ranging from upbeat and joyful to depressed, flat, or melancholy at other times. Teenagers frequently need more solitude or alone time, which is completely acceptable. These emotional ups and downs might occur more frequently and to a greater degree throughout the adolescent years.

Types of Emotions

There are several hypotheses about the wide range of emotions that people may feel. Paul Ekman, a psychologist, identified the following six as being universal feelings:

Happiness: Many individuals aspire to be happy since it is a positive emotion that is accompanied by a feeling of well-being and satisfaction. Smiling or using a cheery voice are frequent ways to convey happiness.

Sadness: Everybody occasionally feels sad. Someone may cry, keep silent, or retreat from others to convey their unhappiness. Sadness may take several forms, such as grief, hopelessness, and disappointment.

Fear: Fear may speed up the pulse rate, send thoughts racing, or make you want to run away. It could be a response to real or imagined dangers. Some individuals engage in activities like viewing scary movies, going on roller coasters, or skydiving to experience the adrenaline rush that comes with dread.

Disgust: Moral disgust may occur when someone sees another person doing something they find immoral or distasteful.

Anger: Anger may be shown on the face by frowning, screaming, or acting violently. Finding a healthy outlet for your anger can prevent it from hurting you or other people, yet anger may inspire you to make changes in your life.

Surprise: Surprise can be pleasant or unpleasant. When you are startled, you could open your lips or gasp. The fight-or-flight response may be triggered by surprise just like by fear.

"Young brains are sometimes represented as stews of hormones and irrationality, yet the

judgments they make are frequently quite sensible and need more thought."
By Daniel Siegel

How dopamine can mess with emotions

The dopamine-using brain circuits, a chemical crucial to forming our drive for pleasure, become more active during adolescence.
Adolescents are drawn to thrilling events and exhilarating feelings because of this increased dopamine release, which begins in early adolescence and peaks halfway through. According to research, dopamine levels are even lower during rest, but they

rise as a result of experience, which may help to explain why unless they are involved in some interesting and unique activities, teenagers may report feeling "bored."

Adolescents may experience a strong sensation of being alive when they are actively participating in life due to this elevated natural dopamine release. Additionally, it may cause people to ignore or undervalue possible dangers and negative effects in favor of concentrating only on the advantages they are certain will come their way.

Teens experience the three most significant manifestations of the brain's increasing drive for reward during adolescence. One is simply an increase in impulsivity when actions are taken without careful deliberation. To put it another way, an urge always prompts action. When we pause, we may consider alternatives to the dopamine-driven desire that is currently pounding on our minds. It takes time and effort to tell an urge to calm down, so it's simpler to just resist acting on it. Having said that, spending the time necessary for processing—for contemplation and self-awareness—becomes extremely vital when we are teenagers since the need for reward is stronger and more compelling than before. We are living our lives entirely on the gas pedal with no brakes if any thought is instantly followed by an action without any thought.

The known increase in our vulnerability to addiction is a second way that increased dopamine release throughout adolescence impacts us. Dopamine is released as a result of all addictive behaviors and drugs. Teenagers are more inclined to explore new things and to respond to these experiences by releasing a lot of dopamine. Alcohol, for instance, can cause the production of dopamine, which might cause us to feel motivated to consume beer, wine, or hard liquor. Our dopamine levels fall when drinking stops. After then, we feel compelled to take more of the substance that stimulated our dopamine systems.

Chapter 2

Factors that can affect a teen emotions

Physical, emotional, social, and psychological factors may all play a role in your child's emotional ups and downs; no one factor alone is to blame. Frequently, neither you nor your kid will be able to pinpoint the exact cause of how they are feeling.

why do emotional ups and downs occur?

Physical elements

Adolescence is a time of significant bodily change for young individuals.

They may feel self-conscious or uncomfortable about their changing bodies, or they may just desire more time and space for themselves. Children who seem to be maturing sooner or later than their peers might have emotional reactions to these physical changes.

The amount of sleep your youngster needs is another physical aspect. Teenagers require 8 to 10 hours of sleep every night, and how much sleep they receive might have an impact on their mood.

Your child's physical health will benefit from regular, wholesome meals and enough exercise, which may also aid with emotional ups and downs.

Brain factor

The teenage years bring about a lot of changes in the brain.

For instance, your child's body produces sex hormones as a result of brain changes. These hormones cause bodily changes as well as emotions of sex and romance. For your kid, these brand-new emotions may be intense and perhaps perplexing.

Your child's brain will continue to develop until they are in their early 20s. The prefrontal cortex, the final portion of the brain to mature, is intimately linked to the regions in charge of regulating and managing emotions. This implies that your kid could struggle to restrain some of their more intense feelings, and it might seem that they respond to circumstances more emotionally than they did in the past. They are still figuring out how to handle and communicate their emotions maturely.

Emotional and social influences

Your child's mood might be affected by new ideas, feelings, acquaintances, and obligations.

As they progress toward independence, your kid is learning how to deal with more challenges on their own. Additionally, your kid is spending more time in their heads than they used to and is preoccupied with

problems like friendships, school, and family ties.
Your child's mood might also be affected by stressful familial events.

assisting adolescents to experience more highs than lows. There are a few things you can do to support your kid in experiencing more highs than lows.

The first step is identifying what your youngster already finds enjoyable. Some examples of these include engaging in a favorite sport, hanging out with old friends, enjoying music or making it, painting, making digital material, and so on. Maintaining these activities will provide your kid a sense of stability and grounding and give them a foundation from which to explore new interests.

You may assist your kid in discovering new pursuits that will test them, enable them to establish new objectives, and allow them to make new friends. These can include taking up a new hobby or joining a different social group. Instead of selecting these activities for your kid, you may try listening to what they say about what they like and hate to glean hints about potential new interests.

Assisting young people with emotional ups and downs

Your youngster will inevitably experience low or depressed moods. To assist your kid deal with the ups and downs, you may take a variety of actions.

Letting your kid know that you have flat spots from time to time is one of the finest methods to do this. Additionally, it's crucial for your kid to know that you'll be there for them if they're struggling or feeling down. Simply stating, "I can tell you're having a terrible day," might be helpful.

Keeping in touch with your kid

You'll be able to identify the reasons for your child's emotional ups and downs more readily if you stay in touch with them and pay attention to what's happening in their lives. The ideal moments for your kid to share things with you might sometimes be during routine, daily activities like taking them someplace or watching TV together.

Allowing your youngster some room

Youth are becoming more independent and taking on new challenges. Try to allow your youngster time or space to reflect on fresh feelings and experiences while they're doing this. Make sure your youngster knows you are there if they need to chat.

Withholding solutions

If there is a problem, it might be nice to talk about solutions with your kid, but they must be ones that they contributed to and feel like they "own." If your kid believes they contributed to the solution, they are more inclined to attempt it.

Another important life skill that your kid will develop through practicing is problem-solving. You may demonstrate that you appreciate your child's involvement in choices that will have an impact on their life by investing time and effort into helping them improve their problem-solving abilities.

collaborating to develop coping mechanisms One of the major tasks of adolescence is learning to deal with and regulate emotional ups and downs on one's own. And you can assist your kid in learning this critical life skill.

Making a list of "mood busters" with your kid is one method to do this. Your youngster can do these actions to feel better. For instance:

receiving a hug from you, taking a quick stroll, listening to happy music, or a favorite song.
Your youngster should have a few choices on the list so they may experiment and choose what works best.
Children's emotional resilience is mostly shaped by their early experiences and interactions with their families. Children's desire for stability and ongoing familial bond is essential for their emotional growth and conduct as they become older.

It is widely accepted that childhood and early adolescent experiences play a vital role in later adult behavior including how we cope with pressure and disappointment.

As adults, we often act out the roles we were taught as kids and teenagers, which greatly influences how we see the world. Our surroundings will seem to be full with dangers if we feel uneasy in our personal relationships and anxious about the future.
In other words, negative "scripts" or reactions that are learnt early in life are often difficult to modify as we become older (but not always impossible).

A parent or guardian who actively encourages a child's development of good life scripts makes an investment in that child's emotional future by imparting personal coping mechanisms that may be used in the event of unpleasant or possibly unstable emotions.

There are two key practical ingredients.
The first involves creating personal tactics for enhancing emotions; examples include being aware of physical signals and mastering physiological relaxation techniques.

The second is the modeling of constructive thinking or thc ability to check fears, anxieties, and irrational feelings with calm convincing self-argument – the development of rational, positive thinking.

This underlying approach has become the basis of much current counseling and psychotherapy and is central to techniques that use a solution focus to promote emotional health – the goal being to build resilience, not fragility.

Experiences from early life are essential for emotional well-being.

Primary attachment and bonding to a parent or caretaker during the first year of a child's life are crucial because they create initial trust and security and provide the groundwork for later emotional development. This is a topic that has been extensively investigated and documented.

The biggest influences on younger children continue to be their ongoing familial experiences.
Family tragedies including illness, unemployment, death, and family dissolution may have devastating repercussions, particularly if the youngster

feels that the family structure itself is in danger.

Education also has a significant impact.

The ability to participate with classmates, feel fostered and encouraged by the school environment, and keep up with classwork are all experiences that help people feel "connected" to their school and teachers, which in turn helps to lessen ambiguity or uncertainty.

Security issues in one area may and often do affect it in another, however, sometimes a passive youngster might mask their mental tension, especially if they are obedient students. Typically, the youngster does exhibit some behavioral clues that point to an emotional issue.

Several more elements affect young children's emotional development in addition to family and school. These include one's genetic makeup, contacts with outside social and sports groups, and contemporary communications technologies like computers and television.

These influences remain important as children become older, particularly those that are most strongly linked to self-image and the drive for increased individualization, including adolescent fashion and pop culture. The pressure on young people to be a marketable products in our consumer-driven world is aggravating this predicament.

A young person who was emotionally resilient as a youngster will have an edge when dealing with difficulties in later life.

Signs of emotional fragility

Young children often exhibit regression in behavior when put under stressful circumstances. Withdrawal, sulking, being too dependent on a parent, recurrent nightmares, bedwetting, violent play at school and/or with siblings, and specific fears or phobias are just a few examples of behaviors that may be present.

In most cases, parents and teachers can tell when something is wrong.

As children go through their many developmental phases, changes in behavior and interests are very natural; parents should take this into account while examining any recent particular behavior.

More subtle changes at school and among peers may be seen in older children and early adolescents. These can include declining motivation and grades in school, a discernible decline in interest in friends and social activities, or unsettling changes to eating and/or sleeping schedules.

What can parents/guardians do?

Positive communication is one of the most essential components of healthy, well-adjusted families because it teaches children the importance of interdependent family support.

When a kid does well, praise should be given, and positive reinforcement should be used in place of criticism if a child falls short of expectations.

Parents should constantly attempt to avoid criticism that doesn't work to promote desirable behavior, even if it might be difficult to cope with children's misbehavior.

Home consistency is crucial for emotional growth since it helps lessen any personal ambiguity or uncertainty. For instance, a young kid must understand the norms and limits that govern the family to internalize these concepts into their psyche. The older kid values the security that comes with routinely occurring events.

Modern couples often experience divorce and separation; to minimize the consequences of diverse parenting styles, separated parents must stay in touch concerning their children. In family law legislation today, the idea of shared parental responsibility has been codified.

Parents may encourage mutuality and help children adapt to new settings by taking an active interest in their academic and social activities.

With so many external constraints on parents nowadays and the easy accessibility of "babysitters" like television and video games, it may be easier than ever to be a "passive" parent. Nintendo will probably not be able to replicate the difficulties kids have in interpersonal interactions daily.

Some people would be surprised to find that teens do want their parents to keep an eye on them, despite complaints to the contrary.

Some teenagers seem to distance themselves from their families and stop talking about their friends and extracurricular activities. Parents may feel anxious and even irate about this.

Teenagers often don't purposely conceal information from their parents. Their actions are a result of their desire to create a "new" identity.

– one that sets them apart from childhood and all that comes with it, including relying on their parents. Teenagers continue to be quite dependent despite this, as every parent is aware.

Although the parent's role often has to adapt to this developmental period, it is crucial to retain keen parental attention. Although parents often tell me their children don't want them around, many teens I encounter in private practice criticize their parents' seeming lack of interest in them.

Conflicts often seem to begin with opposing attitudes and interests. Teenagers may exhibit violent, careless, and egotistical behaviors as a means of pushing the limits set by their parents.

Avoiding the temptation of giving in to this sort of behavior is important for parents. It is preferable to maintain composure and consistency while being open to listening without feeling obligated to concur.

Instead of complaining about how much the world has changed, parents are more likely to connect with their kids if they speak honestly about their attitudes and sentiments as teens. (The generation gap has been for a while; it is good to keep in mind that time does not stand still; when today's teens become tomorrow's parents, views and interests will have once more altered.)

Dealing with unpredictable emotions throughout adolescence becomes more crucial than ever.

Teenagers, who often attempt to manage the feeling by "holding it in," are less likely than younger children to reveal or show emotional problems. This may be a challenge for parents who are torn between wanting to remain a confidant and respecting the child's developing desire for seclusion, particularly if there are unspoken issues.

The majority of young people react to parental displays of love and attention, but often in settings and at times of their choice. On the route to activities and athletic events, the conversation may be extremely free and flowing in the vehicle but may be muffled at home. This could be the case because there is little eye contact and perhaps background music, which creates a psychologically safe space (at least for the teenager).

There are times when a parent finds it hard to "get through," and the family is quite worried about the child's behavior. When this occurs, taking action outside of the immediate family, whether it be via the support of a loving relative, an adult friend, or a professional may be beneficial.

It should always be kept in mind that raising teens involves a lot of confidence in oneself, common sense, an open mind, flexibility, patience, and patience.

If our sons and daughters see these qualities in us, they are more likely to acquire them in themselves.

The environment in which a kid grows up and the kind of people they are exposed to are two aspects that have an impact on how they behave socially. Similar to this, kids must be taught how to manage and comprehend their emotions if they are to become emotionally powerful.

The social and cultural influences of one's family and environment have a significant impact on one's ability to articulate their emotions. The caregiver-child interaction enables a kid to express both good and negative emotions in a way that is acceptable in society and culture.

Emotional changes in adolescence

Moods and feelings
Your youngster may exhibit strong emotions and powerful sentiments, and their moods may seem erratic. Your child's brain is still learning how to regulate and express emotions in a mature manner, which contributes to these emotional ups and downs.

The capacity for empathy
Your youngster will get more adept at reading and comprehending other people's emotions as they mature. However, while they are learning these abilities, your kid may sometimes misinterpret body language or facial emotions. This indicates that they

could require assistance figuring out how other people are feeling.

Self-consciousness

How teens feel about their appearance often has an impact on their self-esteem. Your youngster may get self-conscious about their looks as they grow. Your youngster may also make physical comparisons with classmates and pals.

Decision-making

Your youngster may go through a phase when they often behave without thinking. Your youngster is still learning how to make decisions and that their actions might sometimes have hazards attached to them.

Fostering the emotional growth of adolescents.

Emotional transitions are a component of growing up for your kid. You may play a significant part in your child's social and emotional development. For your kid to have good social and emotional development, they must have strong bonds with their family and friends.

Here are some suggestions to assist you in fostering your child's emotional growth:

Set an example:
You may serve as an example of how to have a good connection with your friends, kids, spouse, and coworkers. Your kid will pick up valuable lessons from partnerships that value empathy, respect, and constructive dispute resolution. Additionally, you may

serve as an example of how to handle disagreement and challenging emotions in a constructive manner. For instance, there will be occasions when you feel irritable, exhausted, and unsociable. You may remark, "I'm weary and cross," rather than withholding affection from your kid or getting into a fight. I think I can't speak right now without becoming angry. Can we talk about this after dinner?

Find out who your child's pals are.
You may monitor your child's social interactions by getting to know their friends and making them feel welcome in your house. Additionally, it demonstrates your understanding of the significance of your child's friendships to his or her sense of self.

You may be able to direct your youngster toward other social groups if you're worried about their buddies. The reverse outcome, though, may occur if you forbid companionship or criticize your child's pals. In other words, your kid could want to hang out with the buddies you've forbidden even more.

Pay attention to your kid's emotions.

During these years, active listening may be a very effective strategy for enhancing your kid's emotions. When your kid wants to chat, you must put down what you are doing and pay attention. When your kid acts in a certain manner, express your feelings to them, since this will teach them how to recognize and react to emotions. It also serves as an example of constructive and pleasant interpersonal interactions. Simply stating, "I was incredibly thrilled when you asked me to your school performance"

Discuss dating, sex, and sexuality.

Talking openly and without judgment about sex, relationships, and sexuality with your kid may help you build their trust. But instead of having a major conversation, try to find regular occasions when you may simply bring up these topics.

It's often wise to find out what your youngster already understands when these circumstances arise. Give the facts and correct any falsehoods if any. These discussions may also be used to discuss acceptable sexual behavior as well as topics like consent, sexting, and pornography. Additionally, let your youngster know that you are always accessible to discuss any issues or queries.

Concentrate on the good

There may be instances when you and your kid seem to be in constant disagreement or when your youngster exhibits extreme moodiness. It is beneficial to concentrate on and emphasize your child's social and emotional development during these periods. You may commend your kid, for instance, for being a good friend, having a diverse range of hobbies, or making an effort in school.

Chapter 3

How emotions work and understanding them

Researchers have discovered that certain types of ideas often result in particular emotions. For instance, someone who believes they are in danger is likely to experience fear. Or, a person would likely feel delighted if they thought, "I just received what I desired." Or, a person could feel sad if they think, "I just lost something I care about." Last but not least, someone who believes "My buddy just treated me unjustly" is likely to get furious.

Scientists have found that emotions are often caused by ideas that provide answers to problems like these:

Is what occurred unexpected?

Was what occurred amusing?

Will, what transpired make it simpler or more difficult for me to achieve my goals?

Can I influence what occurs after that?

Will I be able to handle what transpired?

Does what occurred line up with my ideas of what is good and wrong?

Was it my fault or was it someone else's?

Depending on how your mind responds to these many inquiries, you will experience various emotions when a certain incident occurs. For instance, if your bike suddenly broke, you would likely feel worse if you believed there was nothing you could do to repair it (i.e., if you believed you had no control over the situation). Or, if your closest buddy had just moved away, you probably wouldn't be as unhappy about it if you thought you could handle it and make other friends. Alternatively, if you believe that not sharing is bad, you could get upset when someone doesn't.

But have you ever had a feeling that you couldn't place? Sometimes individuals experience emotions even when they are unaware of any associated ideas. This may be hard to comprehend. However, researchers have shown that sometimes your brain might inadvertently evoke a feeling. This implies that without your awareness, your brain may take note of anything in your circumstances and cause an emotional response. In reality, according to scientific research, our brains do a wide range of tasks that we are unaware of. We refer to this as "unconscious processes." For instance, even though you're unaware of it, your brain is now in charge of numerous bodily functions, including those of your heart and stomach. Try to pay attention to what is occurring in your present circumstances and ask yourself the seven distinct questions listed above the next time you experience an emotion you don't understand. You may be able to understand your feelings better after reading this.

Understanding your emotions

What emotions are you experiencing as you read this book right now? Are you enquiring? Are you hoping to discover anything about yourself? Are you satisfied since it's a school assignment even if you're not very interested in it, or are you bored because it is? Perhaps you're preoccupied with something else, such as excitement about upcoming activities for the weekend or sadness over a recent split.

These kinds of emotions are typical of human nature. They inform us of our circumstances and assist us in determining how to respond.

Since we are infants, we can perceive our emotions. Young children and infants show their emotions by facial expressions and/or activities, such as laughing, hugging, or crying. They experience and display emotions, but they are unable to identify them or explain why they are experiencing them.

We become better at comprehending emotions as we get older. We can recognize our feelings and express them verbally rather than just responding as young children do. We grow better at understanding our feelings and the reasons behind them with time and practice. We refer to this ability as emotional awareness. Knowing what we need and desire (or don't want) is made easier by emotional awareness. Our interpersonal interactions improve as a result. That's because being conscious of our emotions may make it easier for us to express how we feel, avoid or settle disputes, and get through challenging emotions.

Some people just have more emotional sensitivity than others. The good news is that everyone can increase their emotional awareness. It just requires practice. Emotional awareness is the first step in developing emotional intelligence, a talent that may help people thrive in life, thus it's worth the effort.

Here are some fundamentals about emotions:

Emotions change with time. Most people experience a wide range of emotions during the day. Some only survive a short while. Others could stick around and develop a mood.

Emotions may range from being moderate to be quite strong. An emotion's strength may vary depending on the circumstance and the individual.
There are excellent and poor methods to express (or act on) emotions, even if there are no good or bad feelings. Understanding emotions are the basis for regulating

emotions, which is the ability to learn how to express emotions in appropriate ways.

Positive feelings include joy, love, assurance, inspiration, jubilation, curiosity, gratitude, and inclusion. Other feelings, such as anger, resentment, fear, humiliation, guilt, sadness, or worry, might come out as more negative. Emotions, both good and bad, arc natural.

All emotions reveal something about who we are and the circumstances we are in. But sometimes it's challenging for us to accept how we're feeling. We may criticize ourselves for having certain emotions, such as jealousy, for example. It's best to pay attention to how we genuinely feel rather than telling ourselves that we shouldn't feel that way.

Avoiding unpleasant emotions or trying to seem as if we don't feel the way we do might backfire. If we don't confront them and attempt to understand why we feel that way, it's tougher to get over challenging emotions and allow them to pass. You don't have to linger on your feelings or speak about them all the time. Simply said, emotional awareness is the ability to acknowledge, appreciate, and accept your emotions as they arise.

Increasing Emotional Intelligence

Emotional awareness enables us to understand and accept who we are. What steps can you take to increase your emotional awareness? Start with the following easy steps:

Make it a practice to pay attention to your feelings in various circumstances throughout the day. Making preparations to go someplace with a companion may cause you to experience the excitement. or that you have anxiety before a test. When you are listening to music, seeing art, or receiving compliments from friends, you could feel at peace. Simply take note of every feeling you are experiencing and give it a mental name. Even though it just takes a little moment, this is an excellent practice. Keep in mind that every feeling fades and provides a place for the next one.

Rank the intensity of the emotion. Once you've recognized and named an emotion, go one step further: On a scale of 1 to 10, where 10 is the most powerful sensation, rate how strongly you experience the emotion.

Let your loved ones know how you're feeling. This is the ideal approach to practicing verbalizing feelings, a skill that makes us feel more connected to friends, partners, parents, coaches, or anybody else. Make it a habit to express your emotions to a friend or member of your family every day. You can share something personal or just a feeling you experience often.

Teenagers who give in to their emotions risk losing perspective on what is true because emotions have a way of obscuring the broader picture.

Teenagers often deal with situations beyond their control, which may lead to anxiety, which is rooted in dread. Fear may be caused by uncontrollable things. Teenagers may find it helpful to learn how to identify and then let go of what cannot be managed since it is crucial to know what can be controlled and what cannot. Undoubtedly, it is much simpler to say than to execute this!

Understanding emotions can help you choose how to react to them in the most effective manner, which is one solid reason to do so. It is crucial to first determine if your feelings fit the present scenario before deciding how to react. When they take place under the appropriate circumstances, emotional responses may be beneficial. For instance, if you are afraid of snakes, your fear will assist you to avoid being bitten and avoid being around them. Or, if you get furious when someone treats you unfairly, your rage may persuade the offender to stop being cruel. Or, if your loved ones see your grief in the wake of a friend's departure, they will understand that you need their love and support.

However, if they occur in the wrong circumstances, these same feelings may sometimes be counterproductive. For instance, your relationship may suffer if you are upset with a buddy because he accidentally wounded you. Or, if you stay home from class because you are so anxious about a test, this might prevent you from passing that class. Or, if you grieve for too long after a buddy leaves, it could be more difficult for you to meet new people.

It's important to pay attention to your feelings and to practice identifying them. You'll be able to solve difficulties and recover from illnesses more quickly if you do this. It also helps to reflect on past instances of sadness, fear, and anger, and ask yourself what you have learned from them and how you would respond if a similar circumstance arose in the future.

Understanding emotions may also be beneficial since it might make it easier for you to comprehend others. Maybe you've seen someone get upset or outraged in a circumstance, but you weren't able to understand why. After reading this book, you are aware that these folks likely have different perspectives on this topic than you do. They presumably have different life experiences than you have, which is why they see the issue differently. Generally speaking, if you spend some time attempting to comprehend a person's thinking and prior experiences, this will likely also help you understand why that person feels the way they do.

Our brains season our lives with salt and pepper, but emotions are more than that. Life may be unpleasant if taken too far. Life may be bland if it isn't well-seasoned.

Emotions are thus crucial. To get the most out of the remainder of the mind, we just need to get to know them, comprehend them, and capitalize on their energy, particularly throughout the adolescent years.

Chapter 4

How to manage negative emotions

Teen life isn't shown in movies. Trying to combine school, schoolwork, your family, and your social life is tough. Trauma and drama must also be dealt with.

Teenagers often want to blend in. They want to decide for themselves and go into uncharted territory. They sometimes take chances. While some people establish their identities with ease, others have trouble discovering their calling. Teens who are having trouble regulating their emotions may display these symptoms. This indicates that they are unable to control or regulate their intense emotions. They may have depression symptoms if they are not good at controlling their emotions. For instance, they could experience times of dread or melancholy. According to research, adolescents who struggle to control their emotions are more likely to engage in a range of hazardous activities.Through a number of circumstances, teenagers develop the ability to control their emotions. Social media, culture, friends, religion, parents, schools, or authority individuals are all sources of information for them. Parents are

among the factors that have the biggest influence.
Teens learn by observing. They learn by listening. Parents may not be aware that kids pick up on emotional management skills just by observing them.

It might be challenging to teach youngsters how to manage their tough emotions. However, assisting them in understanding their feelings will also help them avoid experiencing depressed symptoms.

Positive feelings do exist. Consider feelings like pleasure, happiness, intrigue, enthusiasm, grattitude, love, and satisfaction. These pleasant feelings are pleasant. Negative emotions, such as melancholy, rage, loneliness, envy, self-criticism, fear, or rejection, may sometimes be challenging and even painful.

This is especially true when we feel something negatively very strongly, protractedly, or excessively.

Negative emotions are impossible to avoid, though. Everyone feels them from time to time. Even if they could be difficult, we can learn to handle them.

- Step 1: Identify the Emotion
  It takes work to become aware of and understand your emotions. Make sure to pay attention to your body as well as your sentiments. With certain emotions, you could experience physical sensations; for instance, your

muscles might tighten up or your face might get heated.

- Be aware of how you feel. Try to put a name to your unpleasant emotions, such as rage, when they arise.
  For example:
- That girl Jenna in my project group makes me so mad!
- I feel so jealous whenever I see that person with my ex—that lady or that guy. Every time I have to pass those bullies, I become nervous.
- Don't hide how you feel from yourself. You might not want to broadcast your feelings to other people (like your ex, for example, or that girl in your project group who is making you mad). But don't suppress your feelings entirely. It is far better to just

acknowledge the emotion than to try to hide it or to lose control and erupt.

Know the causes of your feelings. Find out what occurred to cause you to feel the way you do.

For example:

Whenever we do group projects, Jenna finds a way to take all the credit for other people's work.

Our teacher thinks Jenna is the star of the team, even though she never has her ideas.

My ex's flirtatious behavior with other individuals serves as a reminder that I still have emotions for him or her.

The bullies don't specifically target me, but I worry when I see what they do to other people

Don't blame.

It's not the same as assigning blame for how you feel to someone or anything just because you can identify and explain your feelings. The female who steals credit for your efforts may not even be aware that she is doing it, and it's unlikely that your ex is dating someone new as a strategy to get even with you. You control how you feel when these things occur. Your emotions are there to assist you make sense of what's happening.

Recognize that all of your feelings are normal and reasonable. Don't criticize yourself for your feelings. It's common to experience these. Don't be harsh on yourself; acknowledging how you feel might help you move on.

Do Something

You may determine if you need to communicate your emotion after you've given what you're experiencing some thought. Sometimes just realizing how you feel is sufficient, but other times you'll want to take action to feel better.

Consider your options for expressing your feelings. Do you need to calmly approach someone else right now? Discuss your feelings with a friend. maybe go for a run to get rid of the emotion?
For instance:
Expressing my displeasure to Jenna won't help anything and can make her feel superior. But my gut tells me to stay away from another circumstance when she usurps someone else's laborious efforts.

I'll keep my head held high around my ex, then I'll put on some depressing music and have a big weep in my room to help me let go.
It's a warning indication that they've gone too far when I'm afraid to be near those bullies. Maybe I should discuss my situation with a school counselor.

Find out how to alter your mood.
You'll want to change your attitude from being unhappy to being happy at some time. Otherwise, you risk having a fixed perspective on how awful things are, which will only make you feel worse. Even if you don't feel like it at the moment, try to do the things that make you happy. After a breakup, you may not feel like going out, but taking a stroll or seeing a hilarious movie

with friends might help you get over that bad attitude.

Develop an optimistic attitude.

Happiness and well-being are produced by having positive sensations. Make it a practice to acknowledge and concentrate on the positive aspects of your life, even the tiny ones, like the compliment your father gave you for tidying up his room or how delicious the pizza you prepared for supper. Even when you're having a difficult day, focusing on the positive aspects of life might help you change your emotional equilibrium from bad to good.

Seek assistance

Discuss your feelings with your parents, a responsible adult, or a friend. They may aid in your emotional exploration and provide you with new perspectives. Nothing except the support of someone who accepts you for who you are may make you feel more understood and cared for.

Exercise

Engaging in physical exercise aids the brain's natural chemical production of mood-enhancing substances. Exercise may also help you relieve tension and prevent you from harboring unfavorable emotions.

Get Assistance With Difficult Feelings

Sometimes a difficult feeling is impossible to overcome, no matter what you do. You may want further support if your grief or anxiety lasts for more than a few weeks, or if you feel so angry that you fear harming yourself or others.

Speak with a therapist, parent, trustworthy adult, or school counselor. Therapists and counselors have received training in helping clients learn how to overcome difficult emotions. They may provide you with several suggestions and guidance to make you feel better.

The teenage years may be challenging for a variety of reasons. Teenagers often want to blend in. They want to decide for themselves and go into uncharted territory. They sometimes take chances. While some people establish their identities with ease, others have trouble discovering their calling. Teens who are having trouble regulating their emotions may display these symptoms. This indicates that they are unable to control or regulate their intense emotions. They may have depression symptoms if they are not good at controlling their emotions. For instance, they could experience times of dread or melancholy. According to research, adolescents who struggle to control their emotions are more likely to engage in a range of hazardous activities.

Through several circumstances, teenagers develop the ability to control their emotions. Social media, culture, friends, religion, parents, schools, or authorized individuals are all sources of information for them. Parents are among the factors that have the biggest influence. Teenagers learn knowledge through watching. They learn their knowledge through listening. Parents may not be aware that kids pick up on emotional management skills just by observing them.

It might be challenging to teach youngsters how to manage their tough emotions. However, assisting them in understanding their feelings will also help them avoid experiencing depressive symptoms.

It is simple to neglect to instruct teenagers in emotional management. A lot of parents believe that by the time their children are in high school, they should already be able to control their emotions. Consequently, many parents neglect to instill emotional intelligence in their children. Research reveals the reverse, nevertheless. Teenagers require increasing amounts of assistance in understanding their emotions due to the continual flow of media and social trends.

Teach teenagers how to manage their emotions if they are experiencing problems. Emotional coaching is the name of this technique. Parents may help their teenagers navigate their emotions in several ways:

Show that you can tolerate your unpleasant feelings by setting an example.

Inform your adolescent verbally that his or her feelings do not determine their value as people.

Allow your adolescent to freely express their emotions without displaying any symptoms of embarrassment.
When your adolescent expresses grief, anxiety, or rage, gently accept the reality of those feelings so they know you are not disputing their validity.

Tell your adolescent again that you completely understand how they are feeling.

Teach your adolescent to record his or her emotions in a notebook so that they may be processed.

Talk to your adolescent about potential remedies to make them feel better.
Teach your adolescent when to express certain unpleasant emotions and when it is

inappropriate to do so. For instance, it is preferable to express intense emotions privately rather than in front of others.

The most essential thing is to let your adolescent know that you love them, regardless of how much pain, rage, or terror they are experiencing. The strongest indication to them that you accept them for who they are is your love for them, regardless of how they may be feeling.

These direct coaching techniques benefit teenagers in numerous ways. They are more inclined to form wholesome partnerships. Teenagers often acquire emotional intelligence and self-control. Additionally, their self-esteem, level of stress, and academic performance seem to be improving. Teenagers who get emotional support are less likely to develop depressive symptoms.

Conclusion

You can better control your emotions if you are aware of them. Adolescence is a period of significant social, emotional, and relational changes. Teenagers' emotional coping strategies are shaped by a range of influences. These factors shape the attitudes that affect how adolescents see themselves. One of the main factors influencing teenagers' emotional development is their parents. As a result, parents need to be more conscious of the impact that their actions might have on teenage mental health. Parents may effectively guide their children through difficult emotions that teenagers endure. In the end, this may aid in preventing further adolescent depressive symptoms. Social and emotional intelligence in adolescence is largely dependent on positive relationships between parents.

www.ingramcontent.com/pod-product-compliance
Lightning Source LLC
LaVergne TN
LVHW052051160826
845678LV00015B/3165

* 9 7 9 8 8 4 6 4 8 9 6 4 6 *